QUESTIONS AND ANSWERS
ABOUT
SPACE

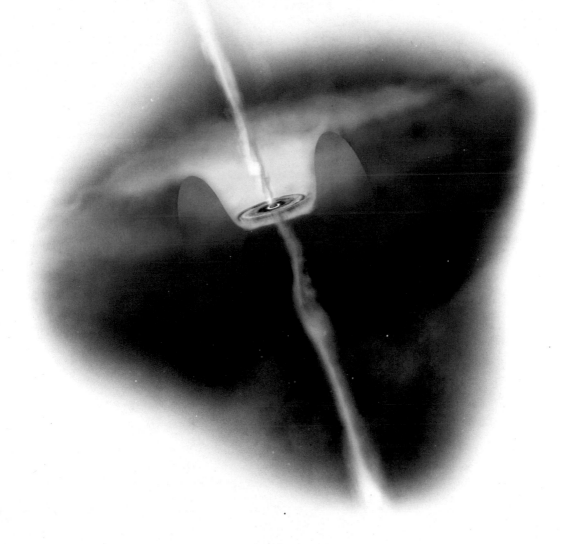

Capella

This edition published in 2008 by Arcturus Publishing Limited,
26/27 Bickels Yard, 151-153 Bermondsey Street,
London SE1 3HA

ISBN 978-1-84837-157-6

Designers: Q2A India and Jane Hawkins
Editors: Ella Fern, Fiona Tulloch and Alex Woolf

Printed in China

Contents

Introduction

The universe is a vast, mostly empty space and is more than 15 billion years old. Within it are at least 100 billion galaxies and an even larger number of stars. One of those galaxies is the Milky Way, and one of the stars in the Milky Way is our Sun. Like all stars, the Sun is a giant ball of gas and dust that gives out heat and light. The Sun, together with all the planets, asteroids, comets and meteors in orbit around it, make up the solar system.

In this book, you will discover many fascinating facts about space, the galaxies, the stars, the solar system and human attempts to explore the cosmos. How big is the universe? How did the Milky Way get its name? What is a black hole? What's the weather like on Mars? And will it ever be possible to live in space? You will find the answers to these and many other questions in the pages of this book.

Galaxies

The universe is a huge open space made up of billions of galaxies and an even larger number of stars. Our galaxy is called the Milky Way. Our solar system, including the Sun, the planets and their moons, forms just a tiny part of the Milky Way.

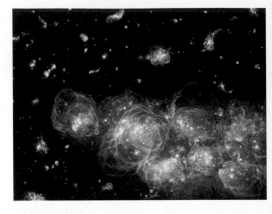

▲ **Early universe**
Scientists think that the early universe was a dense cluster of matter, that has kept expanding from the Big Bang until now and is continuing to expand.

Quick Q's:

1. What is the Big Bang theory?

The Big Bang theory suggests that the universe as we know it today was created after a huge explosion or "bang." Georges Lemaitre proposed the theory of the Big Bang in 1927, and in 1929 Edwin Hubble expanded on his work.

2. Which is the largest galaxy?

Scientists do not know exactly. The largest galaxies we know of are giant elliptical (oval) galaxies located in the middle of a whole group of galaxies. One of the largest is in the central galaxy in the cluster Abell 2029.

3. How big is the Milky Way?

The Milky Way is huge. It takes the Sun about 250 million years to orbit once around the center of the Milky Way.

4. What is Messier Object 31?

The Andromeda Galaxy is also known as Messier Object 31, or M31. This galaxy is more than twice the size of Milky Way. But it is still not the largest galaxy we know of.

Q How was the universe formed?

A The universe was born more than 15 billion years ago. It is believed that the universe began as a small ball of fire. This fireball grew larger and larger until one day it exploded, to form the universe that we know.

Q How big is the universe?

A No one knows how big the universe really is. There are at least 100 billion galaxies that we know of. However, this number keeps growing as better telescopes are developed and we see more and more galaxies. On top of that, the galaxies are moving away from each other, causing the universe to expand. Some scientists believe that the universe will never stop expanding, while others think that one day it will begin to shrink until it becomes a fireball again.

Q What is a galaxy?

A A galaxy is a group of billions of stars, dust and gas bound together by gravitational force. A galaxy can either be on its own or in a cluster. Galaxies come in different shapes and sizes. Scientists have divided them into three categories based on their shapes—spiral, elliptical (oval) and irregular (no shape).

▼ **Expanding universe**
Scientists think that stars and other elements in the universe are continuing to move away from each other due to the force of the original Big Bang.

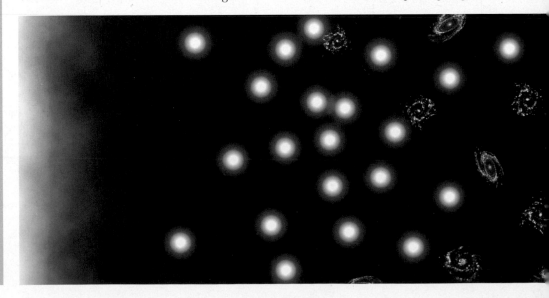

Q How did the Milky Way get its name?

A In ancient Greek and Roman myths, it was believed that the goddess Hera (Juno) spilt milk across the sky and called the white streak it left a "river of milk." The Romans called it *Via Lactea* or a "road made of milk." This is how our galaxy came to be named the Milky Way.

Q Is the Milky Way a part of a cluster of galaxies?

A The Milky Way and three of its neighboring galaxies are part of a larger cluster known as the Local Group (because they are closest to Earth). The neighboring galaxies in the Local Group are called Andromeda, and the Large and Small Magellanic Clouds. Of the 35 galaxies in the Local Group, only these three can be seen with the naked eye.

▶ **Milky Way**
An artist's impression of our galaxy, the Milky Way, based on observations made by modern telescopes. Our Sun is a small star on one arm of the galaxy.

A galactic crash

Sometimes, galaxies crash into one another due to the force of gravity. But the stars in them are too far apart to cause any real damage. Our own galaxy is on a collision course with its neighbor Andromeda. The collision will take place in about five billion years and the two will merge to form an elliptical (oval) galaxy.

Try these too...

Stars (10–11),
The Sun (12–13),
The Planets (14–15),
Comets and Asteroids (24–25)

Stars

A star is a huge ball of gas and dust that gives out both heat and light. When the gases in the star burn out, it dies. A star can live for millions, even billions, of years depending on its size. Each galaxy in the universe is made up of several billion stars.

Q What is a protostar?

A Stars are born in clouds of dust and gases, mainly hydrogen. More and more gas is pulled together by gravity to form a cloud. After a while the cloud begins to spin. This makes the gas atoms bump into each other at high speeds, creating a great deal of heat. As the cloud becomes hotter a nuclear reaction takes place inside, and the cloud begins to glow. This glowing cloud is called a protostar. The protostar continues to contract until it becomes a star.

Q How long does a star live?

A A star glows for millions of years until the gases in its outer layer begin to cool, and the hydrogen in the inner core is slowly used up. The cool outer layer starts to glow red. When this happens the star is called a red giant. The red giant continues to lose its brightness until it fades away. Depending on its size, a red giant may die in an explosion, get compressed to form a black hole or become a white dwarf.

Q What is a white dwarf?

A A small star usually shrinks to form a dense white dwarf. The size of a white dwarf is similar to the size of Earth. There are many white dwarfs in our galaxy but they are too dim to be seen. Sirius B is one of them.

▲ **Protostar**
An artist's impression of the original ball of dust and gases that combine to form a protostar.

Q What is a supernova?

A A supernova is a vast explosion in which an entire star is destroyed. After the explosion, extremely bright light is emitted for several days. Supernovas appear a billion times brighter than the Sun. Sometimes, a supernova explosion can go on for weeks or even months. Supernovas mostly occur in distant galaxies. The last supernova to take place in the Milky Way occurred in 1604. It was observed by the famous astronomer Johannes Kepler. The brightest supernova to be recorded so far is 1993J in the galaxy M81. It was seen on 26 March 1993. But because the stars are so far away, we may see a supernova explosion long after it takes place.

▶ **White dwarf**
An enhanced image of white dwarf stars, which have already shrunk to a size comparable to that of the Earth. These stars are too dim to be detected without modern telescopes.

Q What is a black hole?

A Black holes are extremely compact space objects that were once massive stars. Sometimes a huge star begins to shrink until it is smaller than an atom. This is called a black hole. The center of a black hole is called a "singularity."

▾ **Black hole**
Nobody can actually see a black hole, because the extremely strong gravity inside them does not even allow any light to escape, let alone anything else. This is an artist's impression of what a black hole may be like.

The gravity near this point is so strong that any object that gets too close to the black hole is pulled into it. Even light gets sucked into it, which is why we can't see a black hole. Scientists use special instruments to detect a black hole's presence. They examine the effects it has on the objects near it.

▾ **Dwarf stars**
When stars reach the end of their lives, their fires start to die out, and then they become dwarf stars due to the gravitational pull of the matter inside.

Heavenly pictures

By drawing imaginary lines between the stars in the sky, you will notice the shapes of animals or objects familiar to you. You might see a crab, a dragon, a bear or other patterns. These star patterns are called constellations. Astronomers have identified 88 constellations in all. The more famous ones are the Great Bear, the Little Bear and Orion, also known as the Hunter. The constellations also include characters from Greek mythology and the 12 signs of the zodiac.

Try these too...

Galaxies (8–9),

The Sun (12–13),

The Planets (14–15),

The Moon (22–23),

Humans in Space (26–27),

Communication and Satellites (28–29)

The Sun

Our solar system is made up of the Sun, eight planets, three dwarf planets and many asteroids, comets and other space rocks. The Sun is the largest object in the solar system and is located right at its center. The planets, dwarf planets, asteroids and comets travel around the Sun in an ellipse. Our solar system was formed about 5 billion years ago, and the surface of the Sun is about 4.6 billion years old.

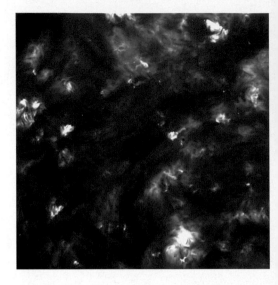

▲ **Flaring up!**
Solar flares on the surface of the Sun. Solar flares were observed for the first time in 1859.

Quick Q's:

1. What are sunspots?

Sunspots are storms on the surface of the Sun. These storms appear as huge, dark spots in satellite pictures and so are called sunspots.

2. How hot is the Sun?

The Sun's surface temperature is about 5,760 °C (10,400 °F), while its center is an incredible 15 million °C (28 million °F)— that is more than 150,000 times hotter than boiling water!

3. How far is the Sun from us?

The Sun is about 150 million kilometers (93 million miles) away from the Earth.

4. What is the corona?

The corona is the glowing atmosphere of the Sun that extends millions of kilometers into space. The corona is 200 times hotter than the Sun's surface!

5. Is the Sun worshiped by people?

The Sun has been worshiped as a god since ancient times by the Greeks, Romans and native Americans.

Q How was the Sun created?

A Before it was formed, the Sun and the rest of the solar system was a huge mass of hot gas and dust called a solar nebula. This nebula spun faster and faster until the clouds of gases, dust and ice particles clumped together and exploded, forming the sun.

Q Why does the Sun glow?

A The Sun is made up of huge amounts of hydrogen and helium gases. Nuclear reactions at the center of the Sun emit a large amount of energy that makes the Sun glow. That same energy travels through space and reaches us as heat and light.

Q What is a solar eclipse?

A A solar eclipse occurs when the Moon comes between the Sun and the Earth, blocking the Sun from our view. In a total solar eclipse, the Moon blocks out the Sun from our view completely. In a partial eclipse, however, a part of the Sun is visible. During an annular eclipse, we can see a small ring of the Sun glowing around the Moon. When the Moon is nearer to the Earth it appears larger and therefore covers the Sun completely, although it is actually much smaller than the Sun. However, in an annular eclipse the Moon is too far away from the Earth to block the Sun out totally and therefore a ring of sunlight is seen.

Q What is a solar flare?

A Sometimes the Sun produces a huge amount of magnetic energy that sends out jets of gas into space. These jets of gas are called solar flares and cause a sudden increase in the brightness of the Sun. Solar flares are often followed by the release of electrically charged particles like protons and electrons. These are called solar winds and are known to travel at a speed of about 500 kilometers (300 miles) per second.

▼ **Blocking the Sun**
In an annular (ring-shaped) eclipse, the Moon covers only the middle portion of the Sun, causing a bright ring of light to appear around the Moon.

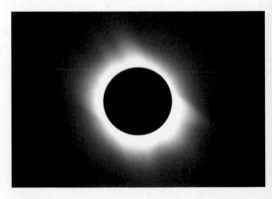

Q Is the Sun really a star?

A The Sun is a medium-sized star known as a yellow dwarf. It is younger and smaller than most stars in the universe, but is very bright and extremely hot. In about five billion years, when all the hydrogen in its core has been used up, the Sun will change into a red giant star. After that, the Sun will evolve into a white dwarf before finally dying out.

Q How did we learn about the Sun?

A We have sent several solar missions into space to study the Sun and its characteristics. The first detailed observations were made by NASA's Pioneer missions that were launched between 1959 and 1968. The Solar Maximum mission of 1980 made a detailed study of solar flares. The Solar and Heliospheric Observatory (SOHO) launched in 1995, has been continuously collecting data regarding the Sun for the last ten years.

In different directions!

The Sun takes about 26 days on average to rotate on its axis. Since it is made up of gas, different parts of the Sun rotate at different speeds. The surface closest to the equator rotates faster than that closest to the polar regions. The Sun's surface near the poles takes almost 36 days to complete one rotation.

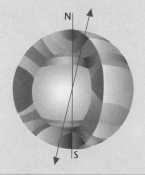

▼ **A joint effort**
The SOHO was launched jointly by the European Space Agency and NASA. For over ten years, SOHO has been studying the outer layers of the Sun.

▸ **Surface of the Sun**
There is constant activity visible on the surface of the Sun, as it pulses and glows due to the heat and light produced by the nuclear reactions within.

Try these too...

Galaxies (8–9),
The Planets (14–15),
The Moon (22–23)

The Planets

Planets are large masses of matter that orbit around a star. Our solar system consists of eight planets—Mercury, Venus, Earth, Mars, which are called inner or rocky planets, and Jupiter, Saturn, Uranus and Neptune, which are the outer planets, or gas giants.

Quick Q's:

1. How did the planets get their names?

All the planets are named after Roman gods. Venus is named after the Roman goddess of love. The surface features of Venus are also named after various goddesses. For example the planet has a deep canyon named Diana, after the Roman goddess of hunting.

2. How many rings do Jupiter and Uranus have?

Jupiter has three thin rings that cannot be seen even with the most powerful telescopes. Uranus has as many as 11 rings.

3. How many moons does Venus have?

Apart from Mercury, Venus is the only other planet in the solar system that has no moon.

4. What about Pluto?

Until recently, Pluto was the ninth planet in our solar system. But in 2006, it was officially reclassified as a dwarf planet, because it is so small and its gravitational field is not as strong as that of the major planets.

Q How were the planets formed?

A After the gaseous cloud called the solar nebula collapsed upon itself due to the strength of its own gravity and formed the Sun, the dust and particles around it clumped together to form the planets. The heat of the Sun melted the ice particles nearby and eventually these rocks grew larger to form the four rocky planets. Some ice particles were too far away from the Sun to be melted. These ice pieces combined with gases to form the planets called the gas giants.

Q What are the features of a rocky planet?

A The rocky planets are made up of rocks and metals like iron and nickel. They are smaller than the gas giants but are very heavy. Because of their weight, the rocky planets rotate much more slowly than the gas giants.

▼ Rocky planets
Among the rocky planets, the Earth appears blue from outer space because over 70 percent of its surface is covered with water.

▲ Birth of planets
The planets in our solar system were born when dust and particles around the Sun clumped together.

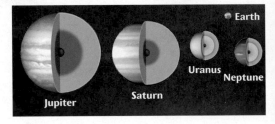

▲ Gas giants
The four outer planets, the gas giants, are much larger than the Earth.

Q What makes gas giants unique?

A The gas giants are bigger in size but lighter, as they are mainly made up of gases and ice particles. In fact, Saturn is so light that it would float if placed in water! Gas giants also spin extremely quickly and they have rings around them. These planets do not have a hard surface. Jupiter and Saturn have a semi-liquid center that is covered by a layer of liquid gas.

Mercury

Venus

Earth

Mars

Q What are the distinguishing features of each of the rocky planets?

A Mercury is the closest to the Sun and therefore its temperature can be as high as 467 °C (873 °F). Venus is covered with carbon dioxide containing droplets of sulphuric acid. This traps the Sun's heat and makes Venus hotter even than Mercury. Mars, the red planet, is considered to be the only planet after Earth where life could exist. As far as we know, the Earth is the only planet that supports life.

Q What are the special characteristics of the gas giants?

A Jupiter is the largest planet. It rotates faster than any other planet and has the most moons. Saturn is set apart by its beautiful rings, made up of dust particles and pieces of ice. Uranus is a strange planet where seasons last for more than 20 years, while Neptune is the windiest planet in the solar system.

JUPITER

1 Amalthea
2 Adrastea
3 Metis
4 Thebe

▲ **Jupiter's moons**
Jupiter, the largest planet in the solar system, has so many moons that we are constantly discovering new ones. This image shows some of the bigger moons and the gossamer rings around the planet.

▼ **The solar system**
The relative sizes of the eight planets and the three dwarf planets are shown in this diagram of the solar system. Jupiter is the largest planet. The Sun, of course, is much larger than any of the planets.

Try these too...

Galaxies (8–9), The Sun (12–13), The Hot Planet (16), The Earth's Twin (17), The Red Planet (18), The King of Planets (19), The Last Planets (20), Dwarf Planets (21), The Moon (22–23), Comets and Asteroids (24–25)

Saturn's moons

At least 46 moons orbit Saturn. Each moon is unique. Enceladus is among the shiniest objects in space. Titan's atmosphere is thicker than Earth's. Here are the big moons, seen from behind the moon Dione.

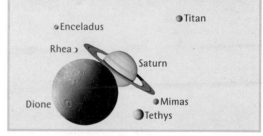

Enceladus
Rhea
Dione
Saturn
Titan
Mimas
Tethys

PLANETS

1 Mercury
2 Venus
3 Earth
4 Mars
5 Jupiter
6 Saturn
7 Uranus
8 Neptune

DWARF PLANETS
9 Ceres
10 Pluto
11 Eris

The Hot Planet

Mercury is the planet closest to the Sun. It is also very small—about the size of Earth's Moon. It is named after the Roman messenger god because it moves very quickly.

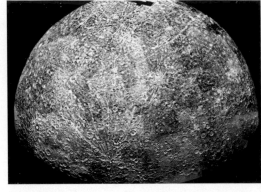

▲ **Sandy surface**
Mercury has a surface that is full of hills and steep canyons, all of it covered with a mixture of sandy substances. The core of the planet is metallic, like all the rocky planets.

Quick Q's:

1. How long does Mercury take to orbit the Sun?

Like all planets, Mercury goes around the Sun in an elliptical (oval) orbit. It takes about 88 days to complete one orbit.

2. How long is a day on Mercury?

Mercury goes around the Sun very fast, but rotates very slowly on its axis. Therefore a day on Mercury is equal to 176 Earth days!

3. Why does Mercury have huge craters?

As Mercury has very little atmosphere, meteors do not burn up in the air. Instead, they fall on the surface, creating huge craters.

4. What color is the sky above Mercury?

If you were to look at the sky from Mercury, even during the day, it would appear black. This is because there is no atmosphere to spread the Sun's light.

5. Which is the largest crater on Mercury?

The largest crater is the Caloris Basin. It is about 1,300 kilometers (808 miles) in diameter. It is also one of the biggest craters in the solar system.

Q Why are nights on Mercury freezing cold, although it's the planet closest to the Sun?

A Unlike Earth, Mercury is not surrounded by a thick protective blanket of air called the atmosphere. This means that the heat from the Sun escapes, leaving the planet freezing at night. While the temperature during the day can be as high as 467 °C (873 °F), at night it drops to -183 °C (-297 °F).

Q What is the surface of Mercury like?

A If you were to land on Mercury, you would find a surface very similar to that of the Moon. It has dust-covered hills and cliffs and is dotted by craters. The planet also has a thick metallic core and a sandy crust.

Q What space probes have been launched to Mercury?

A Mercury, being so close to the Sun, is very difficult to explore. Space probes are unable to withstand the heat of the planet. Only one space probe, Mariner 10, has visited Mercury so far. It photographed nearly half of the planet's surface. A new probe, Messenger, is on its way to Mercury. It was launched on 3 August 2004 and is expected to return, after photographing the whole planet, in March 2012. Another space mission will begin in 2013.

solar panel

Sun shade

TV cameras

◀ **Looking at Mercury**
The Mariner 10 space probe is the only one to have got anywhere near Mercury so far. It is sending photographs of the surface of Mercury regularly now.

◀ **Mercury close-up**
From up close, the surface of Mercury can be seen to be pitted with huge craters. Any meteor that comes near Mercury falls on the surface and creates a crater, as there is no atmosphere to burn the meteor up.

The Earth's Twin

Venus is the second planet from the Sun. It is also Earth's closest neighbor and its size, composition, gravity and distance from the Sun are similar to the Earth's. Venus is so similar to Earth, that it is often considered to be its twin. However, in reality, Venus is very different.

Q Why is Venus hotter than Mercury?

A Venus has a thick atmosphere, much thicker than the Earth's. The atmosphere is mainly carbon dioxide. This greenhouse gas traps large amounts of heat within the planet. That is why Venus is hotter than Mercury, though Mercury is closer to the Sun.

Q Why is a day longer than a year on Venus?

A Venus goes around the Sun at a very high speed. It takes only about 225 days to complete one orbit. However, it spins much more slowly on its axis, taking about 243 days to complete a rotation. Therefore, days on Venus are longer than years.

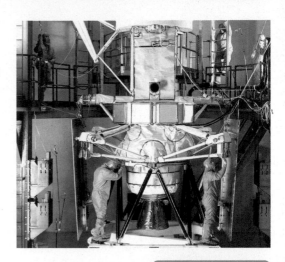

▶ **Mapping Venus**
Scientists have sent a number of space missions to Venus to find out more about its size, atmosphere, interior and surface, especially its volcanoes.

Q Are there volcanoes on Venus?

A There are more volcanoes on Venus than there are on Earth. About 80 percent of the planet's surface is made up of smooth volcanic plains, and there are two major mountain ranges with volcanoes that may be active. The peak of Maxwell Montes, the highest mountain on Venus, lies 11 kilometers (7 miles) above the surface of the planet. Mount Everest rises only about 9 kilometers (6 miles) above sea level.

Try these too...

The Sun (12–13), The Planets (14–15), The Red Planet (18), The King of Planets (22–23), Comets and Asteroids (24–25), Humans in Space (26–27)

▼ **Volcano on Venus**
There is far more volcanic activity inside Venus than inside Earth; so, Venus has many more volcanoes.

Spinning backward

All the planets rotate from west to east on their axes, apart from Venus, which spins in the opposite direction. On the surface of Venus, the Sun appears to rise in the west and set in the east. The planet might have been hit by a huge space rock, reversing the direction of its spin.

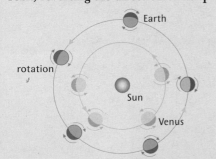

rotation

Earth

Sun

Venus

The Red Planet

Mars is the fourth planet from the Sun and is named after the Roman god of war. It is also called the red planet because it glows red in the sky. The presence of rust (iron oxide) on its surface gives the planet its color.

Quick Q's:

1. Can you see Mars from the Earth?

On a clear night, Mars can be observed with the naked eye. Between July and September the Martian surface can be observed clearly through a telescope.

2. How many moons does Mars have?

Mars has two moons called Phobos and Deimos, which orbit very closely to its surface. Both moons are believed to be asteroids that were captured by the gravity of Mars as they came close to it.

3. Is there life on Mars?

The atmosphere of Mars is 95 percent carbon dioxide, 3 percent nitrogen and 1.6 percent argon. Traces of oxygen and water have also been found. Some scientists have claimed to have found traces of methane. This gave rise to the speculation that there may be life on Mars, since methane is a gas produced by many animals. But other scientists pointed out that methane is also produced by the mineral olivine, which can be found on Mars.

Q **What is the surface of Mars like?**

A The surface of Mars is divided into the northern plains flattened by lava flows, and the southern highlands marked by huge craters. The planet boasts Olympus Mons, the largest volcano in the solar system.

Q **Is there water on Mars?**

A Scientists have found signs of water in rock layers. In 2006, the scientists saw new deposits of sediment on the surface of Mars. These sediments had not been there six years earlier. According to scientists at NASA, this is the strongest evidence so far that water still flows occasionally on the surface of Mars, though other scientists say the sediments could have been deposited by carbon dioxide frost or movement of dust. Samples of the minerals haematite and goethite have also been found in Mars. These minerals are sometimes formed in the presence of water.

▶ **Martian moon**
The two moons of Mars are quite small compared to our Moon. They may be asteroids caught by the gravity of Mars.

◀ **Red planet**
The surface of Mars looks reddish brown due to the presence of iron oxide.

The scientists have also found signs of frozen water near the South Pole of Mars. It is believed that huge floods flowed through Mars about 3.5 billion years ago. The water from the floods may have once collected in huge basins.

Q **Why are seasons on Mars longer than on Earth?**

A Mars and Earth are tilted on their axis in the same way. Therefore, Mars has almost the same kind of seasons as Earth. However, because a Martian year is equal to two years on Earth, each Martian season lasts twice as long as the seasons on Earth.

Q **What kind of weather would you find on Mars?**

A The temperature varies from -140 to 20 °C (-220 to 68 °F). The polar ice caps on Mars increase and decrease in size alternately in winter and summer. Mars also has dust storms, which can cover the entire planet.

▼ **Olympus Mons**
The tallest volcano in the solar system, Olympus Mons towers 27 kilometers (16.88 miles) above the surface of Mars.

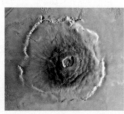

◀ **Look out for Mars**
From 27 August 2006, Earth and Mars have been closer to each other than they have been in the last 60,000 years! It has begun to appear brightly in the night sky, as seen here while looking south-east from Poodle Rock in the Valley of Fire State Park, Nevada, USA. Now Mars will be the brightest object in the night sky after the Moon and Venus.

The King of Planets

Jupiter is the first of the gas giants and the fifth planet from the Sun. It is the largest of all the planets. In fact, more than a thousand Earths could fit inside it!

Q How did Jupiter get its name?

A The planet is named after the king of the Roman gods. It is indeed the king of the planets, not just because of its massive size, but also because it rotates the fastest. It is the fourth brightest object in the sky, after the Sun, the Moon and Venus.

Q How many moons does Jupiter have?

A Jupiter has more than 60 moons. Galileo Galilei, the famous Italian astronomer, saw the four largest moons of Jupiter in 1610. They were named Io, Europa, Callisto and Ganymede. By the 1970s nine more moons were discovered and today we know of 63.

Volcanic moon

Io, one of the four largest moons, lies very close to Jupiter. There is a great deal of pressure on this small moon, since it is constantly being pulled by the gravity of Jupiter and the other large moons. This tug of war generates a lot of heat, so Io is covered with active volcanoes.

Q What is the Great Red Spot?

A Jupiter is a planet of storms. The biggest storm area is called the Great Red Spot. It has been raging for at least 340 years. It is so big that it can be seen from the Earth through a telescope.

Q How many explorations have been made to Jupiter?

A Many explorations have been made to the king of planets. Pioneer 11 took the first close-up images in 1974, studied the atmosphere and detected Jupiter's magnetic field. Space probe Galileo, launched in 1989, orbited Jupiter. In 2000, the Cassini probe took the best ever photos.

▼ **Planet spotter**
The Galileo space probe was the first to make an entire orbit around Jupiter.

Great Red Spot

▲ **Giant ball of gas**
There are constant storms on Jupiter, during which the winds can roar five times faster than the fastest hurricane on Earth. Some of the big storms are seen here in brown.

Try these too...

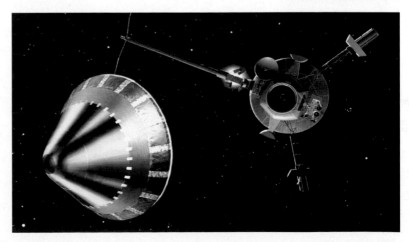

The Last Planets

Next to Jupiter are Saturn, Uranus and finally Neptune. Saturn is the second largest planet in the solar system. Like Jupiter, Saturn and Uranus are made up of gases. All three planets have rings, but it is Saturn's rings that are the most spectacular.

Q Why do Saturn's rings shine?

A Saturn's rings consist of dust particles and pieces of ice that can be quite large. The ice pieces reflect light, causing the rings to shine.

▲ **Saturn's rings**
Saturn has seven large rings, each made up of thousands of smaller rings. These are among the brightest objects you can see through a telescope.

Quick Q's:

1. How big are Saturn's rings?

Saturn's rings can be up to 1 kilometer (0.6 miles) thick and stretch for over 280,000 kilometers (175,000 miles).

2. When were Saturn's rings discovered?

Saturn's rings were first observed by Galileo through a telescope in 1610.

3. Who discovered Uranus?

Uranus was the first planet to be seen through a telescope. It was discovered in 1781 by astronomer William Herschel.

Q What gives Uranus and Neptune their blue color?

A Both planets contain methane. Sunlight is reflected by clouds under the methane layer. Only the blue portion of the reflected light passes through the methane layer, so they appear to be blue.

▼ **Strange rotation**
Uranus rotates from top to bottom as it orbits the Sun.

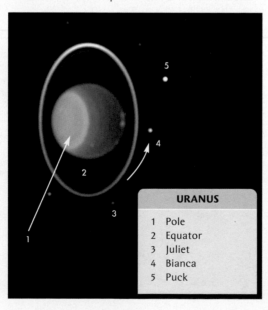

URANUS	
1	Pole
2	Equator
3	Juliet
4	Bianca
5	Puck

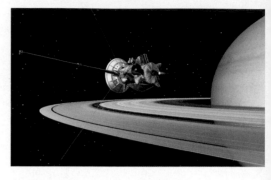

▲ **Probing far**
The Cassini space probe is expected to send us better photographs of the far planets.

Q Why do seasons on Uranus last for over 20 years?

A Uranus has a very peculiar orbit, unique in the solar system. The planet is tilted in such a way that its poles face the Sun directly, so that Uranus spins from top to bottom. It acts like a cylinder that is rotating on its ends instead of rotating on its sides. Scientists believe that another planet-like object might have crashed into Uranus, knocking it over on to its side. The long seasons are caused by the planet's unusual orbit.

Q Are there winds on Neptune?

A Neptune is the windiest planet in our solar system. Winds on this planet can reach speeds of about 2,000 kilometers per hour (1,200 miles per hour). That is more than ten times the speed of the strongest hurricane on Earth.

▼ **Cloudy over Neptune**
The clouds over Neptune are always being blown about by the strong winds on the planet.

Dwarf Planets

In 2006, the International Astronomical Union (IAU) made a decision that changed the way we organize our solar system. The IAU announced the removal of Pluto from the list of planets. They reclassified Pluto as a dwarf planet. Instead of nine, we now have only eight planets in our solar system.

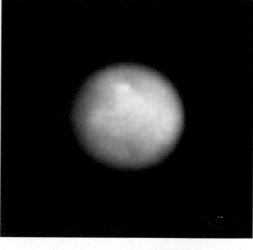

Q How is a dwarf planet different from other planets?

A According to the IAU's new definition, a planet is a space object that orbits the Sun and has a nearly round shape. Its gravity must be strong enough to clear all other space objects (except satellites) out of its orbit. Dwarf planets also orbit the Sun and have a nearly round shape. But other space objects nearby are not cleared by the gravity of the dwarf planets. They are not big enough for their gravitational fields to do this. Dwarf planets are different from satellites, which orbit a planet and not the Sun.

Q How many dwarf planets are there in the solar system?

A Apart from Pluto, Ceres and Eris (UB313) have also been classified as dwarf planets. Until recently, Ceres was called the largest asteroid. It has a diameter of about 950 kilometers (600 miles) and is in the asteroid belt between Mars and Jupiter. Eris is the largest of all the dwarf planets. It has a diameter of about 3,000 kilometers (1,850 miles).

Q Are there any other dwarf planets?

A Scientists are considering including Pluto's moon Charon among the dwarf planets. Charon does not actually go around Pluto—they revolve around each other. The planetoid Sedna and the asteroids Vesta, Pallas and Hygiea are also being considered.

▲ Promoted
Since 2006, Ceres is classified as a dwarf planet. Before that, it was simply the largest of the many asteroids that lie between the orbits of Mars and Jupiter.

◀ Distant Sun
An artist's impression of how the Sun would look from the surface of Eris, the furthest of the dwarf planets in the solar system. The Sun gives almost no heat at that distance and looks like a bright star.

Try these too...
The Sun (12–13), The Planets (14–15), The Red Planet (18), The King of Planets(19), The Last Planets (20), The Moon (22–23), Comets and Asteroids (24–25), Humans in Space (26–27)

Thrown off orbit

Pluto was called the ninth planet for 76 years. After 2006, it was reclassified as a dwarf planet.

1 Sun
2 Mercury
3 Venus
4 Earth
5 Mars
6 Jupiter
7 Saturn
8 Uranus
9 Neptune
10 Pluto

▼ Pluto's moon
Pluto (left) and its moon Charon actually go around each other, rather than Charon going around Pluto. Scientists may soon reclassify Charon as dwarf planet.

The Moon

There are many moons in our solar system, which orbit planets, just like planets orbit the Sun. Earth has one Moon, Mars has two small moons, Mercury and Venus don't have any, while Jupiter has at least 63! The Earth's Moon is made up of rocks, both solid and molten.

Quick Q's:

1. Does our Moon have a scientific name?

Astronomers call the Earth's Moon Luna, to distinguish it from the natural satellites of other planets.

2. If the Moon is cold and dark, how does it give off light?

The Moon does not give off light of its own. It simply reflects the sunlight that falls on it.

3. Why can't we see the Moon during the day?

During the day the bright light of the Sun blocks the soft glow of light reflected by the Moon.

4. What are spring tides and neap tides?

When the Sun, the Moon and the Earth are in a straight line, the gravitational force of the Sun strengthens that of the Moon, causing tides that are higher than usual. These are called spring tides (although they have nothing to do with the season of Spring). When the Sun and the Moon are at right angles to the Earth, weaker tides, called neap tides, are caused. Tides are important to wash away the debris off the coasts.

Q Why is the Moon's surface filled with craters?

A The Moon does not have an atmosphere. Therefore, meteors and asteroids from outer space crash into its surface making craters. Tycho crater, one of the biggest lunar craters, is more than 85 kilometers (50 miles) wide.

Q What does the term "Blue Moon" mean?

A Blue Moon refers to the second Full Moon to appear in a month. It is very rare indeed. There are other definitions of Blue Moon as well, but this is the most widely accepted definition nowadays.

Q How does the Moon cause tides in our oceans and seas?

A Tides are caused by the gravitational force exerted by the Moon on our planet. This force causes the ocean to bulge out in the direction of the Moon, making the tide rise. As the Earth is also pulled toward the Moon, the ocean on the side facing away from the Moon also bulges out. So it is high tide there as well. In the region between the two bulges (high tides) the water level decreases, causing low tides. Tides are higher in the tropics due to the bulge of the equator. Many forms of life on the coast are tailored to the cycle of tides.

▸ **High and low**
The gravitational pull of the Moon on the Earth causes tides in the oceans and seas of the Earth.

▲ **Crescent Moon**
As the Moon orbits around the Earth, we see only a part of it that is lit up by the Sun, depending upon the angle made by the Earth, the Moon and the Sun.

Q Why does the Moon appear crescent-shaped at times?

A The shape of the Moon as seen from the Earth keeps changing. The changing shapes of the Moon are called phases. When the side of the Moon that faces the Earth is turned away from the Sun, we are unable to see the Moon. This phase is called the New Moon. As the Moon travels in its orbit around the Earth, we start to see a small portion of the Moon that is lit up by the Sun. This is called the Crescent Moon. The lit up portion seen by us slowly increases, and we see a Half Moon, then a Three-quarter Moon. When the Moon completes a half orbit around the Earth, we can see the entire disc lit up by the Sun—the Full Moon.

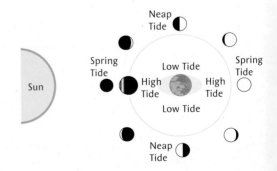

The dark side

Did you know that we see only one side of the Moon at all times? This is because the Moon takes the same amount of time to rotate on its axis as it takes to go around the Earth. The side we see is called the near side, while the one that is never seen is called the dark side. The first time people on Earth got to see the dark side of the Moon was when the first astronauts made an orbit around the Moon, and took photographs. The astronauts lost touch with Earth when they were on the dark side, because the moon blocked their radio signals.

▲ **Phases of the Moon**
We see different parts of the Moon lit up by the Sun, depending upon how much of the Moon that is lit up is facing toward us or facing away from us. This is repeated in a cycle every 28 days.

Try these too...

The Sun (12–13), The Planets (14–15), The Red Planet (18), The King of Planets (19), Humans in Space (26–27)

Comets and Asteroids

Along with the Sun, the planets and their moons, several other objects made up of small pieces of rock, metal and ice are also a part of the solar system. These objects are asteroids, comets and meteors.

Quick Q's:

1. What are sungrazers?

Some comets crash into the Sun or get so close to it that they break up into tiny pieces. Such comets are called sungrazers.

2. Where are asteroids found in the solar system?

Most asteroids are found in a region between Mars and Jupiter, which is known as the asteroid belt.

3. Do asteroids have moons?

The asteroid Ida has a tiny moon, Dactyl. This was discovered by the spacecraft Galileo in 1993.

4. When will Halley's Comet be seen again?

Halley's Comet takes about 76 years to complete one orbit around the Sun, so it is expected to be seen again in 2061.

5. Why does a comet have a tail?

A comet is made up of ice and other material. As it nears the Sun, these materials heat up. Solar wind and pressure from the Sun's radiation push them outward to form a tail that always points away from the Sun.

Q **Are asteroids planets?**

A When the solar system was formed, some fragments of rock were left spinning in space. These huge space rocks that orbit the Sun are called asteroids. Like other planets, asteroids are also made of metals like iron and have moons. Some of them are called minor planets.

Q **Are asteroids dangerous?**

A An asteroid can be thrown off its orbit by the gravity of larger planets, or if it comes too close to another asteroid. Once it is off its orbit, the stray asteroid often strikes the surface of other planets and moons. This causes widespread destruction and creates huge craters. In fact, some scientists think that an asteroid struck Earth about 65 million years ago, causing the extinction of the dinosaurs.

Q **Are shooting stars really stars?**

A Shooting stars are actually pieces of burning rock called meteors. A meteor is formed when a piece of debris in the solar system, called a meteoroid, enters the Earth's atmosphere. As the meteor rubs against the air in the Earth's atmosphere, it gets hotter and hotter until it burns up in a streak of light.

▶ **A meteor**
We can see a meteor without a telescope when it enters the Earth's atmosphere. Sometimes, a number of meteors are seen within a very short period of time. They leave a streak of light, which disappears very quickly. This is called a "meteor shower," also known as a "meteor storm."

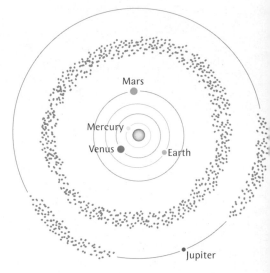

▲ **Asteroid belt**
Most of the asteroids in our solar system can be found in a belt between the orbits of Mars and Jupiter.

Q **How is a comet's tail formed?**

A A comet is a mixture of ice, gas and dust. Like asteroids, they too travel around the Sun. As a comet nears the Sun, the ice on its surface melts and a jet of gas and dust particles is released to form a tail. Comet tails can be as long as 10 million kilometers (6.2 million miles).

Q Do meteors ever fall on Earth?

A Sometimes small fragments of a meteor, called meteorites, crash on to the surface of the Earth. Some are so big that they make craters where they fall. Many meteorites have been found on the Earth's surface. The best known of these is the Barringer Impact Crater in Arizona, USA. This crater was created by an iron meteor that fell on the Earth about 50,000 years ago. The meteor was almost 40 meters (130 feet) in diameter and slammed into the surface at a speed of about 11 kilometers per second (6.8 miles per second), creating a crater that was more than a kilometer wide.

The great Siberian explosion

On 30 July 1908 people living near Lake Baikal in Siberia saw a strange bluish light travel across the sky, followed by a loud explosion and shockwaves that knocked people off their feet. The explosion took place near the Stony Tunguska River and was probably caused by a meteor. It flattened about 80 million trees. The meteor may have broken up about 10 kilometers (6 miles) above the Earth's surface, so it did not leave a crater.

▲ **Huge crater**
The Barringer Impact Crater in the USA was created by a meteorite impact 50,000 years ago.

◀ **Regular visitor**
Halley's Comet orbits around the Sun once every 76 years, and is the most famous comet in human history.

Q Where do comets come from?

A Comets originate in two different areas of the solar system. Comets from the Kuiper Belt beyond Neptune are called short-period, since it takes them less time than other comets to go around the Sun. Comets from the Oort Cloud take as long as 30 million years to complete one orbit and are therefore called long-period comets. There are about a trillion comets in the Oort Cloud. The Oort Cloud itself is at the edge of the solar system, almost a quarter of the way from the Sun to the next star, Proxima Centauri.

Try these too...

The Sun (12–13),

The Planets (14–15),

The Moon (22–23),

Humans in Space (26–27)

Humans in Space

Ever since ancient times, humans have wanted to know more about the skies above them. They invented stories to explain the presence of the stars, the Moon and the Sun. Today, advanced technology helps us to travel into space and expand our knowledge about the world beyond our planet.

▲ **First woman in space**
Valentina Tereshkova was the first woman in space, aboard Vostok 6 on 16 June 1963.

Quick Q's:

1. What was the first living being to orbit Earth?

The first creature to orbit the Earth was a dog named Laika, aboard the Russian spacecraft Sputnik 2 on 3 November 1957.

2. Who was the first person in space?

On 12 April 1961, Russian cosmonaut Yuri Gagarin was the first person to travel in space, aboard the spacecraft Vostok 1. Gagarin orbited the Earth once on this historic flight, which lasted 1 hour and 48 minutes.

3. Which was the first ever space station?

Salyut 1 was the first space station. It was launched on 19 April 1971.

Q How do space shuttles fly into space?

A A space shuttle consists of two rocket boosters, three engines, an external fuel tank and two smaller fuel tanks. It also has an orbiter, which puts the shuttle into orbit. The rockets are used to propel the shuttle into space. When the shuttle is about 45 kilometers (28 miles) high, the rockets fall off into the ocean and the three main engines of the shuttle take over. Just before the shuttle goes into orbit, its engines are shut down and the external fuel tank is discarded.

Q Why can't I fly into space in an aeroplane?

A All objects, even aeroplanes, are glued to the surface of the Earth by gravity. If you wanted to escape this unseen force, you would have to travel at a speed of at least 40,000 kilometers per hour (25,000 miles per hour). Only space shuttles are designed to achieve this speed. A mixture of liquid hydrogen fuel and liquid oxygen is burned under high pressure to help the shuttle's rockets reach this speed and push it out of the Earth's atmosphere into orbit.

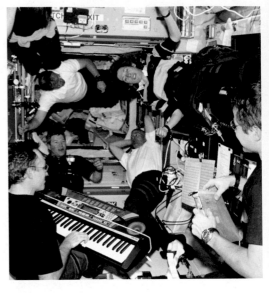

▲ **Weightless games**
On board a spacecraft, astronauts dance in zero gravity, as one colleague holds down a keyboard to play it.

Q Is there no gravity in space?

A All objects in space exert some gravitational force on each other. However, the gravitational force exerted by some objects, like the Moon, is much less than that of the Earth. When humans are in space they float around in the air, because there is not enough gravity to keep their feet on the ground.

▼ **Take off**
These three images show the space shuttle at its base (left), at the moment of take off (center) and on its way to space (right).

Q Could I see the Sun rise and set from space?

A Astronauts aboard a space shuttle orbiting the Earth actually see 16 sunrises and sunsets every day! This is because once in orbit, a space shuttle goes around the Earth at a speed of more than 28,000 kilometers per hour (17,400 miles per hour) and takes only 90 minutes to complete one orbit.

Q Is it possible to live in space?

A Today astronauts spend a great deal of time in space stations. A space station is a floating space base. It is like a spaceship designed so that astronauts can live in outer space for weeks, months or even years at a time. Unlike a spacecraft, a space station cannot take off or land on planets. Other vehicles are used to transport people and materials to and from the station. Space stations are used for studying the effect of long-term space flights on the human body as well as for space research.

Q Is sending humans into space the only way to learn more about it?

A Apart from sending astronauts into space, we also use satellites, probes and telescopes to study space. Like moons, man-made satellites revolve around planets and help us learn more about them. A probe is an unmanned spacecraft sent into space to study objects other than the Earth. We have even put huge telescopes into orbit. The Hubble Space Telescope, sent into orbit in 1990, is the best known among these. It is better to have a telescope in space than on Earth, because then there is no atmosphere to distort the image received by the telescope. However, the biggest telescopes are too big to be sent to space.

▲ **Many sunrises and sunsets**
When astronauts are on board a spacecraft and orbiting the Earth, they are moving much faster than the Earth, so they can see the Sun rise and set many times in a day. The normal human biological cycle can be upset by this, so astronauts are given special medicines to help them sleep.

Try these too...

The Planets (14–15),
The Red Planet (18),
The Moon (22–23)

Looking back in time

The Hubble Space Telescope works like a time machine that can travel into the past. It has taken pictures of the universe when it was barely a billion years old—the universe is at least five billion years old now, though some scientists put its age as high as 14 billion years. The Hubble Space Telescope can look into the past because it takes billions of years for light from the far ends of the universe to reach the telescope. When the light reaches it an image is captured, and we can see what happened in that particular part of the universe long ago.

Communication and Satellites

A satellite is an object that orbits other objects in space. This includes natural satellites like the Moon and artificial satellites made by people. The term satellite came to be used after Galileo Galilei discovered the four main moons of Jupiter.

Quick Q's:

1. When was the first artificial satellite launched?

Sputnik 1 was launched by the then USSR on 4 October 1957. It reached a height of about 250 kilometers (150 miles) and collected information about the furthest reaches of the Earth's atmosphere. Three months later, it burned up completely as it came back to Earth.

2. Who owns the satellites?

The first satellites were owned by countries. Today, with satellites becoming cheaper and doing more work, companies also own satellites. The area on the surface of the Earth covered by the satellite's signal is called its footprint.

3. What is a constellation?

Groups of satellites doing the same kind of work are called a constellation. The Global Positioning System is one such constellation. It is made up of 24 satellites. GPS works in any weather conditions, anywhere in the world, 24 hours a day. A GPS instrument can tell you exactly where on Earth you are.

Q What does an artificial satellite do?

A Artificial satellites have been put to a wide range of uses. Some satellites send and receive television signals so that we can watch many television channels. If there are enough satellites in space, one television programme can be seen all over the world at the same time. Weather satellites help scientists called meteorologists predict what the weather will be like. These satellites can save hundreds of lives by warning fishermen not to sail before a storm, and predicting when a hurricane will strike. Some satellites take photographs of the Earth's surface so that scientists can study changes in the world. This is how scientists know that glaciers that are millions of years old are melting because of global warming. Some others are communication satellites that deal with telephone, fax, internet and computer communications.

▼ Watching a live game
The images captured by the television camera are sent instantly around the world via satellites.

▲ Satellite television
Satellites bring television signals from all over the world instantly into our homes.

Q What is an orbit?

A Artificial satellites are given a definite path around the Earth. The Earth's gravity holds the satellite in a path called an orbit. There are several kinds of orbits. One is Leo or Low Earth Orbit. A Leo satellite circles 160–480 kilometers (100–300 miles) above the Earth's surface. It has to travel very fast to avoid being sucked back to the Earth by gravity. Leos travel at about 28,164 kilometers per hour (17,500 miles per hour) and can circle the Earth in less than two hours. Medium Earth Orbit or Meo satellites are placed 9,656–19,312 kilometers (6,000–12,000 miles) above the Earth. They are often used for communications of all kinds. Geos or Geostationary Earth Orbit satellites circle the Earth in 24 hours, which is the time the Earth takes to rotate once on its axis. So they seem to be fixed above one spot on the Earth. Geo satellites orbit 35,859 kilometers (22,282 miles) above the Earth. They carry television signals across the world, telephone calls between countries and internet messages. They also help predict the weather.

Q How does the satellite get into space?

A A satellite is launched into space on a launch vehicle which is driven by a rocket engine. There are special launch stations for satellites like Cape Canaveral in the USA, Baikonur in Kazakhstan, Kourou in French Guiana and Xichang in China. To start with, launch stations were run by countries or national organizations. Nowadays there are large private companies that also run some launch stations and provide the service of launching a satellite on a commercial basis. These launch stations must be far from human habitation so that the falling launch vehicle lands in water or on desolate land. Some satellites are launched from a portable platform on the Pacific Ocean. The launch vehicle's rockets carry the satellite into a temporary orbit. The rockets and the launch vehicle drop off. Then the satellite is ready to take off on its own motor. When it reaches its permanent orbit, the antennae and solar panels open up and the satellite starts sending and receiving signals.

Q What is a Comsat?

A Communication satellites or Comsats help in long distance communication by receiving and redirecting radio, television and telephone signals. Today, satellites provide a cheaper and better global communication network compared to many land networks. Comsats help large countries like China keep in touch with their remotest parts. They also help countries like Indonesia, which is a country of 13,677 islands, stay connected much more effectively than would have been possible with wires and telephone poles. Navigation satellites provide information for navigation on Earth. They provide signals to moving objects, helping them identify their exact location. These satellites are mostly used by the military and provide information on speed, distance from target or destination and travel time.

▲ **Orbiting the Earth**
A satellite with its solar panels extended orbits the Earth.

◀ **Satellite signals**
Dish antennae are used to receive satellite signals.

Try these too...

The Moon (22-23),
Humans in Space
(26-27)

Satellites for tomorrow

Since 1968, research has been conducted to develop solar power satellites or SPS. The project has been delayed by the high costs to build it. Once taken to a High Earth Orbit, it will beam solar power to Earth for use in place of fossil fuels like coal and petroleum, which are getting depleted quickly.

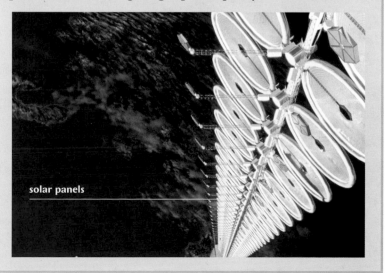

solar panels

Index